MIND-BLOWING EXTREME SPORTS FACTS

100 Insane Feats from the World's Most Daring Athletes

FELIX GRAYSON

Copyright © 2025 by MindSpark Publishing

All rights reserved. No part of this book may be reproduced, stored in a retrieval system, or transmitted in any form or by any means—electronic, mechanical, photocopying, recording, or otherwise—without the prior written permission of the publisher, except in the case of brief quotations embodied in critical articles or reviews.

This book is intended to provide general information on the topics discussed and is not intended as a substitute for professional advice. Every effort has been made to ensure accuracy, but the author and publisher assume no responsibility for errors, omissions, or contrary interpretation of the subject matter.

Published by MindSpark Publishing.
Cover design by MindSpark Publishing.

CONTENTS

Before We Dive In... 8
Introduction 10
The Skydiver Who Broke the Sound Barrier 13
The Cyclist Who Rode Off a Cliff 15
Surfing a 101-Foot Monster 17
The Skater Who Jumped the Great Wall 19
The Marathon Swimmer Who Beat the Ocean 21
Climbing Without a Rope... or Fear 23
Snowboarder Survives an Avalanche Ride 25
The Wingsuit Flight Through a Cave 27
The Ultra Runner Who Ran 350 Miles Nonstop 29
The Skier Who Fell 1,000 Feet and Lived 31
Riding Waves in a River of Lava 33
Skydiving Without a Parachute 35
Motorcycling Across a Tightrope 37
The Cliff Diver Who Jumps from 90 Feet 39
The Man Who Skied Down Everest 41
Kayaking Off a 189-Foot Waterfall 43
Ice Climbing a 300-Foot Frozen Waterfall 45
The Rollerblader Who Jumped Between Roofs 47
Scaling Skyscrapers Without Ropes 49
The Man Who Ran a Marathon in Antarctica 51
The BMX Backflip Over the Thames 53

The Cliff Jumper Who Set a World Record 55
The BASE Jumper Who Leapt from Burj Khalifa 57
Swimming Under a Frozen Lake 59
Jumping Over a Moving Formula 1 Car 61
Running a Marathon in the Death Zone 63
The Skater Who Bombed Lombard Street 65
Paragliding Over an Active Volcano 67
The Desert Cyclist Who Rode for 7 Days 69
Tightrope Walking Between Hot Air Balloons 71
The Snowboarder Who Outran an Avalanche 73
The Free Diver Who Went 702 Feet Deep 75
Skiing Down an Active Volcano 77
The Parkour Jump Over a Moving Train 79
The Skydiver Who Flew With a Jetpack 81
Riding a Bike Across a Canyon Gap 83
The Runner Who Crossed a Continent 85
The Highliner Who Walked Above Rio 87
The Motocross Leap Over a Football Field 89
Kayaking Through a Glacial Ice Cave 91
Snowkiting Across the South Pole 93
The Barefoot Climb of Kilimanjaro 95
Climbing a Waterfall With No Ropes 97
The Longest Underwater Bike Ride 99
The Skydive Into a Volcano Crater 101
The Ultra Swimmer Who Crossed Four Channels 103
Skateboarding Down a 60-MPH Hill 105

Climbing a Skyscraper With Suction Cups 107
Running a Marathon in the Sahara Desert 109
The BASE Jump From an Iceberg 111
The Man Who Paraglided Over Everest 113
Surfing Inside a Live Hurricane 115
The Longest Slackline Walk Over Water 117
The Skier Who Launched Off a Cliff Blindfolded 119
Running a Marathon… in a Volcano 121
The BMX Trick That Defied Physics 123
The Longest Underwater Breath Hold 125
Parachuting Into a Soccer Stadium 127
The Climber Who Hung From a Flying Helicopter 129
The Snowboarder Who Rode an Active Volcano 131
The Ice Swimmer Who Dove Below the Arctic 133
Jumping a Dirt Bike Onto a Moving Train 135
Running Across an Entire Frozen Lake 137
The High-Dive From a Helicopter 139
The Urban Climber Who Hung by One Hand 141
Sandboarding Down a Live Volcano 143
The Windsurfer Who Crossed the Atlantic 145
The Skier Who Backflipped Off a Cliff 147
The Man Who Ran a Marathon Backward 149
Riding a Zipline at 100 MPH 151
The Cyclist Who Rode the Death Road 153
The First Skydive Without a Parachute 155
The Climber Who Slept on a Cliff 157

Running a Marathon in the North Pole 159
The Longest Free Solo Slackline Walk 161
Snowmobiling Across the Arctic Ocean 163
BASE Jumping Into an Underground Cave 165
Riding a Mountain Bike Across a Crane 167
The Longest Swim in a River 169
The Skater Who Did a Loop on a Skybridge 171
Surfing a Wave for Over 3 Minutes 173
The Wingsuit Pilot Who Flew Through a Ring 175
Ice Climbing a Melting Glacier Arch 177
The Ultra Race Through a Jungle 179
The Skydive With a Stunt Plane Loop 181
Climbing a Dam With Bare Hands 183
Riding a Jet Ski Across the Atlantic 185
The Skier Who Jumped Over a Road 187
Paddleboarding Around an Entire Country 189
The Longest Highline Over Active Traffic 191
Cliff Diving From a Hot Air Balloon 193
The Ultra Cyclist Who Rode Around the World 195
Climbing an Iceberg With Ice Axes Only 197
Kayaking Off a Snow-Covered Cliff 199
The BASE Jump Off a Moving Truck 201
The Deepest Scuba Dive Ever Recorded 203
Riding a Unicycle Across a Canyon 205
The Longest Swim in Antarctica 207
The Skater Who Landed the First 1080 209

The Ultimate Triathlon Across Continents 211
Conclusion 212
Acknowledgements 214
About the Author 216

BEFORE WE DIVE IN...

Did you know that this is just **one** of many **mind-blowing** books waiting to be discovered?

What if I told you there's a **world of jaw-dropping, unbelievable, and downright bizarre facts** across **sports, science, history, mysteries, and more**—each one packed with stories that will **challenge what you thought you knew?**

EVER WONDERED WHAT IT'S LIKE TO...

- Witness **record-breaking Olympic moments** that defy human limits?

- Explore **real-life conspiracy theories** that sound too wild to be true?

- Discover **unsolved mysteries** that still leave experts baffled?

- Learn about **billionaires, stock market**

crashes, and money secrets?

- Find out how **robots, AI, and space travel are shaping the future?**

- Experience the **most extreme sports, legendary battles, and shocking events?**

This is just the beginning. The **100 Mind-Blowing series** covers it **all.**

WANT TO SEE WHAT'S NEXT?

Go to **FelixGrayson.com** and explore the **growing collection** of books and audiobooks that will **entertain, amaze, and keep you coming back for more.**

Curiosity doesn't stop here—this is just the beginning. What will blow your mind next?

INTRODUCTION

Welcome to *100 Mind-Blowing Extreme Sports Facts*, a collection built to make you say, "They actually did *what*?" From gravity-defying stunts to near-impossible endurance feats, this book dives headfirst into the wildest, most adrenaline-fueled moments ever caught on camera—or barely survived.

Have you ever heard of someone jumping out of a plane without a parachute? Or riding a bike across a crane high above the city? How about climbing a skyscraper with suction cups or skiing down an erupting volcano? These aren't scenes from an action movie—they really happened, and they're all waiting for you inside.

Each fact has been chosen to shock, amaze, and maybe even inspire a little awe. Whether you're a thrill-seeker, a curious reader, or just someone who loves a good "you won't believe this" moment, there's something here for you. Read it from start to finish or flip to a random page—either way, you're in for a wild ride.

So strap in, hold tight, and prepare to explore the bold, bizarre, and downright mind-blowing world of extreme sports. Just remember: don't try any of this at home. Let's dive in.

Mind-Blowing Extreme Sports Fact #1

MIND-BLOWING EXTREME SPORTS FACT #1

THE SKYDIVER WHO BROKE THE SOUND BARRIER

Felix Baumgartner jumped **from space—and lived to tell the tale.**

In 2012, the Austrian daredevil ascended to the stratosphere in a helium balloon and then *jumped* from an altitude of **128,100 feet**—roughly 24 miles above Earth. During freefall, he reached speeds of **843.6 mph**, becoming the **first human to break the sound barrier without a vehicle.** He plummeted for 4 minutes and 20 seconds before deploying his parachute, landing safely in the New Mexico desert.

The stunt wasn't just extreme—it was history-making, pushing the boundaries of what the human body can endure at the edge of space.

Mind-Blowing Extreme Sports Fact #2

MIND-BLOWING EXTREME SPORTS FACT #2

THE CYCLIST WHO RODE OFF A CLIFF

In 2013, Canadian mountain biker **Kelly McGarry** pulled off one of the most jaw-dropping feats in extreme sports history: a **backflip over a 72-foot canyon** during the Red Bull Rampage in Utah. What made it even more insane? The narrow dirt path, deadly drop-offs, and the fact that one wrong move meant certain disaster.

With a GoPro strapped to his helmet, McGarry launched himself off a cliff, rotated backward in mid-air, and **stuck the landing like it was no big deal**—earning him global fame and one of the most-watched mountain biking videos of all time.

Mind-Blowing Extreme Sports Fact #3

MIND-BLOWING EXTREME SPORTS FACT #3

SURFING A 101-FOOT MONSTER

In 2013, Brazilian surfer **Carlos Burle** rode what is believed to be a **101-foot wave** off the coast of Nazaré, Portugal—one of the most dangerous and unpredictable big-wave spots on Earth.

Facing a wall of water taller than a ten-story building, Burle carved across the wave's face with unbelievable control and courage. What made the moment even more dramatic? Just **minutes earlier, he had rescued fellow surfer Maya Gabeira**, who nearly drowned attempting a similar wave.

Burle's ride wasn't just about records—it was about survival, timing, and pure guts in the face of nature's fury.

Mind-Blowing Extreme Sports Fact #4

MIND-BLOWING EXTREME SPORTS FACT #4

THE SKATER WHO JUMPED THE GREAT WALL

In 2005, skateboarding legend **Danny Way** did the unthinkable: he **jumped over China's Great Wall** on a skateboard—without even using a ramp to land.

Launching himself down a massive roll-in tower, Way hit speeds of over 50 mph before soaring across the ancient structure. Not only did he make the jump successfully, but he **did it five times**—*despite breaking his foot during warmups!*

The stunt blended ancient history with modern daredevilry, cementing Way's legacy as one of the most fearless skaters of all time.

Mind-Blowing Extreme Sports Fact #5

MIND-BLOWING EXTREME SPORTS FACT #5

THE MARATHON SWIMMER WHO BEAT THE OCEAN

In 2013, endurance swimmer **Diana Nyad** became the **first person to swim from Cuba to Florida** *without a shark cage*—at the age of **64**.

She swam **110 miles** through jellyfish-infested, shark-populated waters for nearly **53 hours straight**. After four failed attempts over three decades, Nyad finally conquered the treacherous Florida Straits on her fifth try, fueled by sheer willpower and a mantra: *"Find a way."*

It wasn't just a swim—it was a battle against the limits of the human body, and a triumph 30 years in the making.

Mind-Blowing Extreme Sports Fact #6

MIND-BLOWING EXTREME SPORTS FACT #6

CLIMBING WITHOUT A ROPE... OR FEAR

In 2017, climber **Alex Honnold** stunned the world by **free soloing El Capitan**, a 3,000-foot vertical rock face in Yosemite National Park—with **no rope, no harness, and no room for error.**

For nearly four hours, Honnold scaled sheer granite using only his hands, feet, and absolute mental focus. One slip would've meant instant death. His climb was later featured in the Oscar-winning documentary *Free Solo*, capturing what many consider the **most dangerous athletic feat ever recorded.**

It wasn't just climbing—it was redefining what's humanly possible on a wall.

Mind-Blowing Extreme Sports Fact #7

MIND-BLOWING EXTREME SPORTS FACT #7

SNOWBOARDER SURVIVES AN AVALANCHE RIDE

In 2011, professional snowboarder **Xavier de Le Rue** was filming in the Alps when he triggered a massive avalanche—and was **buried alive while wearing a helmet cam.**

The footage shows de Le Rue getting swept down the mountain like a ragdoll, completely engulfed in snow. Miraculously, his avalanche airbag deployed, and he was able to **dig himself out—uninjured.**

Even after being pummeled by nature's fury, he kept riding. His survival wasn't just luck—it was a masterclass in preparation, calm under pressure, and experience in high-stakes terrain.

Mind-Blowing Extreme Sports Fact #8

MIND-BLOWING EXTREME SPORTS FACT #8

THE WINGSUIT FLIGHT THROUGH A CAVE

In 2011, Finnish wingsuit pilot **Jokke Sommer** pulled off a stunt that looked straight out of a video game: he **flew through a narrow mountain cave**—at over **100 mph.**

Wearing a wingsuit that turned his body into a human glider, Sommer launched from a cliff in the Alps and **threaded the needle through a rock arch barely wider than his wingspan.** One miscalculation would've meant instant impact, but he soared cleanly through, capturing the flight on a helmet cam that later went viral.

It wasn't just flight—it was precision, speed, and bravery in perfect sync.

Mind-Blowing Extreme Sports Fact #9

MIND-BLOWING EXTREME SPORTS FACT #9

THE ULTRA RUNNER WHO RAN 350 MILES NONSTOP

In 2005, ultra-endurance athlete **Dean Karnazes** ran **350 miles without sleeping**—*in one continuous run.*

Starting in San Francisco and ending well into California's Central Valley, Karnazes pushed through **three straight days and nights**, battling hallucinations, blisters, and brutal fatigue. No rest, no naps—just pure forward motion.

Fueled by energy gels, protein shakes, and the occasional slice of pizza mid-run, he shattered expectations of human endurance. When asked why he did it, his answer was simple: *"Because I can."*

Mind-Blowing Extreme Sports Fact #10

MIND-BLOWING EXTREME SPORTS FACT #10

THE SKIER WHO FELL 1,000 FEET AND LIVED

In 2006, extreme skier **Jamie Pierre** was filming in the backcountry of Wyoming when he accidentally triggered an avalanche and **fell over 1,000 feet down a steep mountain face.**

Tossed like a ragdoll through rocks and snow, Pierre miraculously **survived with barely a scratch**—even though he wasn't wearing a helmet. The fall was caught on camera and stunned the skiing world.

He later brushed it off, saying, *"It was a wild ride."* For most people, it would've been their last. For Pierre, it was just another day in the mountains.

Mind-Blowing Extreme Sports Fact #11

MIND-BLOWING EXTREME SPORTS FACT #11

RIDING WAVES IN A RIVER OF LAVA

In 2016, French daredevil **Fred Fugen** surfed a *wave of molten lava*—yes, actual lava—on a modified board during an expedition in the Democratic Republic of the Congo.

Wearing a special heat-resistant suit and surrounded by a support team, Fugen danced just **inches from flowing magma** in one of the planet's most hostile environments. The stunt was part lava surfing, part stunt science—and all completely insane.

It blurred the line between sport and survival, and no one's tried to top it since.

Mind-Blowing Extreme Sports Fact #12

MIND-BLOWING EXTREME SPORTS FACT #12

SKYDIVING WITHOUT A PARACHUTE

In 2016, stuntman **Luke Aikins** jumped out of a plane at 25,000 feet—**without a parachute**—and lived to tell the tale.

Wearing only a wingsuit, Aikins plummeted toward Earth at terminal velocity and **landed in a giant net** barely the size of a baseball diamond. The net was suspended 20 stories high to cushion his fall, and there was zero room for error.

It was the **first-ever successful skydive without a chute**, and it pushed the very concept of freefall to its absolute extreme.

Mind-Blowing Extreme Sports Fact #13

MIND-BLOWING EXTREME SPORTS FACT #13

MOTORCYCLING ACROSS A TIGHTROPE

In 2010, French stuntman **Julien Dupont** took motocross to new heights—literally—by **riding his dirt bike across a tightrope** suspended high above the ground in Lyon, France.

Balancing on a steel cable just inches wide, Dupont carefully throttled forward with dizzying drops on either side. With no safety net below, a single wobble could've spelled disaster. Yet he maintained perfect control, completing the stunt with style—and a few tricks for good measure.

It wasn't just balance—it was high-wire insanity on two wheels.

Mind-Blowing Extreme Sports Fact #14

MIND-BLOWING EXTREME SPORTS FACT #14

THE CLIFF DIVER WHO JUMPS FROM 90 FEET

Professional cliff diver **Orlando Duque** has leapt from heights of up to **90 feet**—*nearly nine stories tall*—into just **16 feet of water.**

With perfect form and zero fear, Duque dives from cliffs, bridges, and platforms worldwide, twisting through the air at speeds over **50 mph** before slicing into the water like a knife. One mistake could mean serious injury—or worse—but his consistency and grace have made him a legend in the sport.

It's not just diving—it's controlled freefall from the sky.

Mind-Blowing Extreme Sports Fact #15

MIND-BLOWING EXTREME SPORTS FACT #15

THE MAN WHO SKIED DOWN EVEREST

In 2000, Slovenian adventurer **Davò Karničar** became the **first person to ski down Mount Everest** from summit to base—**without taking off his skis.**

Starting at 29,035 feet, Karničar navigated sheer ice, deadly crevasses, and razor-thin ridges, all while descending the world's tallest mountain. The entire run took just over 4 hours, but it was the result of years of training and surgical precision.

Most climbers struggle just to survive Everest. Karničar turned it into a high-speed downhill course.

Mind-Blowing Extreme Sports Fact #16

MIND-BLOWING EXTREME SPORTS FACT #16

KAYAKING OFF A 189-FOOT WATERFALL

In 2009, Brazilian kayaker **Pedro Oliva** paddled off the edge of **Salto Belo**, a thunderous waterfall in Brazil measuring **189 feet tall—taller than Niagara Falls.**

Launching over the brink in his kayak, Oliva dropped like a missile into the raging pool below. He surfaced seconds later, miraculously unharmed, and casually raised his paddle in triumph.

It shattered the world record for the highest waterfall descent by kayak—and redefined what's survivable in whitewater.

Mind-Blowing Extreme Sports Fact #17

MIND-BLOWING EXTREME SPORTS FACT #17

ICE CLIMBING A 300-FOOT FROZEN WATERFALL

Extreme climber **Will Gadd** made history in 2015 by **ascending a 300-foot frozen waterfall**—*inside* the Grand Canyon.

Using ice axes and crampons, Gadd scaled the towering, vertical wall of ice formed by a rare freeze along a cliffside spring. The ice was fragile, unpredictable, and melting fast, making every swing and step a high-stakes gamble.

The climb was so risky, it had never been attempted before—and may never be repeated. It was a fleeting moment of icy perfection, captured in one breathtaking ascent.

Mind-Blowing Extreme Sports Fact #18

MIND-BLOWING EXTREME SPORTS FACT #18

THE ROLLERBLADER WHO JUMPED BETWEEN ROOFS

In the early 2000s, French inline skater **Taïg Khris** stunned the world by **leaping between two six-story buildings**—on rollerblades.

The death-defying gap, set up in downtown Paris, left no margin for error. Khris hit top speed down a ramp, launched across open air, and landed cleanly on the opposite rooftop.

But he didn't stop there—he later set a world record by launching off the Eiffel Tower's first platform, landing on a massive ramp below.

This wasn't street skating—it was *urban flight.*

Mind-Blowing Extreme Sports Fact #19

MIND-BLOWING EXTREME SPORTS FACT #19

SCALING SKYSCRAPERS WITHOUT ROPES

French climber **Alain Robert**, nicknamed the "French Spider-Man," has scaled over **100 skyscrapers—without any ropes or safety gear.**

He's climbed landmarks like the **Burj Khalifa**, the **Eiffel Tower**, and **New York's Empire State Building**, using only his hands, feet, and sheer nerve. Often arrested at the top, Robert views each ascent as a personal and philosophical challenge, not just a stunt.

One slip would mean a fatal fall—but that's exactly what makes him climb.

Mind-Blowing Extreme Sports Fact #20

MIND-BLOWING EXTREME SPORTS FACT #20

THE MAN WHO RAN A MARATHON IN ANTARCTICA

In 2002, Irish endurance athlete **Richard Donovan** became the **first person to run a marathon at the South Pole**, braving **-40°F temperatures** and bone-chilling winds.

Wearing multiple layers and battling frostbite risks with every step, Donovan completed the 26.2-mile course on snow and ice, where even breathing felt like inhaling razors. He later went on to run marathons on **all seven continents in just seven days**, but it all started in the coldest place on Earth.

When most people bundle up—he ran.

Mind-Blowing Extreme Sports Fact #21

MIND-BLOWING EXTREME SPORTS FACT #21

THE BMX BACKFLIP OVER THE THAMES

In 2005, UK BMX legend **Kye Forte** launched off a custom ramp and **backflipped his bike over the River Thames** in London—clearing over **60 feet of open water.**

With only a split-second of airtime and a narrow landing ramp waiting on the other side, the margin for error was razor-thin. One miscalculation and he would've ended up in the river—or worse.

Forte stuck the landing, adding his name to the list of riders who turned urban landscapes into jaw-dropping stunt arenas.

Mind-Blowing Extreme Sports Fact #22

MIND-BLOWING EXTREME SPORTS FACT #22

THE CLIFF JUMPER WHO SET A WORLD RECORD

In 2015, Colombian daredevil **Orlando Duque** jumped from a staggering **89 feet (27 meters)** off a cliff into a narrow inlet in Acapulco, Mexico—**setting a world record for the highest cliff dive into shallow water.**

The landing zone was just **13 feet deep**, meaning Duque had to enter the water *perfectly vertical* to avoid serious injury or death. With crowds watching from boats and balconies, he nailed the dive with flawless form.

Precision at that height isn't just skill—it's survival.

Mind-Blowing Extreme Sports Fact #23

MIND-BLOWING EXTREME SPORTS FACT #23

THE BASE JUMPER WHO LEAPT FROM BURJ KHALIFA

In 2014, French skydivers **Fred Fugen** and **Vince Reffet** set a world record by **BASE jumping from the top of the Burj Khalifa**—the tallest building on Earth at **2,722 feet.**

After climbing a custom extension to the spire's peak, they launched themselves into the Dubai skyline, freefalling before deploying their parachutes just above the city's skyscrapers. The stunt required months of planning, special permissions, and nerves of absolute steel.

It wasn't just a leap—it was the highest urban jump in human history.

Mind-Blowing Extreme Sports Fact #24

MIND-BLOWING EXTREME SPORTS FACT #24

SWIMMING UNDER A FROZEN LAKE

In 2021, Danish freediver **Stig Severinsen** swam **over 250 feet beneath a frozen lake** in Greenland—**on a single breath** and **without a wetsuit.**

Wearing only swim trunks and goggles, Severinsen glided under the ice sheet in freezing water, battling both hypothermia and the urge to breathe. The entire swim took more than **2 minutes**, and there was no room for error—**surfacing in the wrong spot could mean death.**

It was part endurance, part meditation, and pure mental mastery beneath the ice.

Mind-Blowing Extreme Sports Fact #25

MIND-BLOWING EXTREME SPORTS FACT #25

JUMPING OVER A MOVING FORMULA 1 CAR

In a stunt straight out of an action movie, free runner **Damien Walters backflipped over a speeding Formula 1 car**—*as it raced directly at him at 60 mph.*

Timed to absolute perfection, Walters stood with his back to the oncoming car, then launched into a backflip **at the exact moment it reached him**, soaring over the vehicle with just inches to spare. One mistimed second could've ended it all.

It wasn't just parkour—it was human timing pushed to the edge.

Mind-Blowing Extreme Sports Fact #26

MIND-BLOWING EXTREME SPORTS FACT #26

RUNNING A MARATHON IN THE DEATH ZONE

In 2017, Nepali runner **Mira Rai** completed a marathon-length trail run **above 18,000 feet** in the Himalayas—**deep in the "Death Zone,"** where oxygen levels are dangerously low.

The brutal course wound through snow-covered ridges, glacier fields, and thin air that would leave most people dizzy just standing still. But Rai, a former child soldier turned elite trail runner, powered through with unmatched endurance and grit.

It wasn't just a race—it was a test of survival in Earth's most unforgiving altitude.

Mind-Blowing Extreme Sports Fact #27

MIND-BLOWING EXTREME SPORTS FACT #27

THE SKATER WHO BOMBED LOMBARD STREET

In 2013, downhill skateboarder **James Kelly** tore down San Francisco's famously twisted **Lombard Street** at breakneck speeds, weaving through hairpin turns **without using brakes.**

Armed with just a helmet and nerves of steel, Kelly leaned into each curve at speeds topping **40 mph**, dodging curbs, oncoming traffic, and clueless tourists. The viral video of his run turned him into a legend in the longboarding world.

It was part slalom, part survival—and 100% gnarly.

Mind-Blowing Extreme Sports Fact #28

MIND-BLOWING EXTREME SPORTS FACT #28

PARAGLIDING OVER AN ACTIVE VOLCANO

In 2007, Spanish paraglider **Horacio Llorens** soared directly **over the mouth of an erupting volcano** in Guatemala—while lava bubbled beneath him.

Harnessing thermal updrafts from the volcano's heat, Llorens circled the crater with molten rock glowing below and ash plumes rising all around him. One wrong move or sudden gust, and he could've been pulled straight into the inferno.

It wasn't just flight—it was *dancing with fire in the sky.*

Mind-Blowing Extreme Sports Fact #29

MIND-BLOWING EXTREME SPORTS FACT #29

THE DESERT CYCLIST WHO RODE FOR 7 DAYS

In 2022, ultra-cyclist **Sofiane Sehili** won the **Atlas Mountain Race** in Morocco—**a 745-mile, nonstop race** through scorching deserts, rocky climbs, and unmarked trails.

Sehili rode almost **continuously for 7 days**, sleeping just a few hours total. He endured sandstorms, sub-freezing nights, and brutal heat—all without outside support. His secret weapon? Grit, strategy, and eating on the move.

It was part expedition, part hallucination—and all-out endurance.

Mind-Blowing Extreme Sports Fact #30

MIND-BLOWING EXTREME SPORTS FACT #30

TIGHTROPE WALKING BETWEEN HOT AIR BALLOONS

In 2020, professional slackliner **Rafael Zugno Bridi** set a jaw-dropping world record by **walking a highline between two hot air balloons—over 6,000 feet in the air.**

With nothing but a safety harness and perfect balance, Bridi tiptoed across a narrow slackline stretched between the drifting balloons, surrounded by nothing but sky and clouds. The entire scene looked surreal—like something out of a dream.

It wasn't just a walk—it was floating on a thread above the Earth.

Mind-Blowing Extreme Sports Fact #31

MIND-BLOWING EXTREME SPORTS FACT #31

THE SNOWBOARDER WHO OUTRAN AN AVALANCHE

In 2016, pro snowboarder **Victor de Le Rue** was riding in the French Alps when an avalanche broke loose—**right behind him.**

With no time to stop or escape sideways, he **charged straight down the mountain,** carving at full speed as a wall of snow thundered at his heels. The entire escape was captured on a drone, showing de Le Rue barely outpacing the collapsing slope in a heart-stopping chase.

It was like surfing a mountain that wanted to bury him. And he won.

Mind-Blowing Extreme Sports Fact #32

MIND-BLOWING EXTREME SPORTS FACT #32

THE FREE DIVER WHO WENT 702 FEET DEEP

In 2023, Croatian freediver **Petar Klovar** set a jaw-dropping world record by diving **702 feet deep—on a single breath**, with no fins, tanks, or propulsion.

Descending into the ocean's inky blackness, Klovar relied on pure technique and inner calm to withstand the **immense pressure** and extreme oxygen deprivation. The round trip took over **4 minutes**, pushing the absolute edge of human physiology.

It wasn't just deep diving—it was a plunge into the limits of life itself.

Mind-Blowing Extreme Sports Fact #33

MIND-BLOWING EXTREME SPORTS FACT #33

SKIING DOWN AN ACTIVE VOLCANO

In 2010, Swedish skier **Andreas Fransson** took on one of the most extreme descents ever attempted: **skiing down Chile's active volcano, Cerro San José**, while it **spewed ash and steam.**

The slopes were unpredictable—part snow, part ice, part volcanic rock—and one wrong turn could've led to a fiery plunge or a deadly slide. But Fransson carved his way down with fluid precision, turning chaos into elegance.

It wasn't just a ski run—it was *dancing on the edge of eruption.*

Mind-Blowing Extreme Sports Fact #34

MIND-BLOWING EXTREME SPORTS FACT #34

THE PARKOUR JUMP OVER A MOVING TRAIN

In 2018, British freerunner **Toby Segar** pulled off a stunt that seemed impossible: he **leapt over a moving train**—*mid-run.*

Timing his approach to the second, Segar sprinted alongside the tracks and vaulted over the train as it passed beneath him, clearing the top **by just a few feet.** The move required perfect judgment, explosive speed, and total commitment.

One hesitation and it would've ended very differently. Instead, it became an instant parkour legend.

Mind-Blowing Extreme Sports Fact #35

MIND-BLOWING EXTREME SPORTS FACT #35

THE SKYDIVER WHO FLEW WITH A JETPACK

In 2015, extreme athlete **Yves Rossy**, also known as "Jetman," launched from a helicopter over Dubai and **flew in formation with an airplane—using a custom-built jet-powered wing strapped to his back.**

With four mini jet engines, Rossy soared through the sky at over **120 mph**, performing barrel rolls and dives with stunning control. Unlike traditional skydiving, there was no freefall—**he was flying like a bird**, with real thrust and lift.

It wasn't falling with style—it was *pure human flight*.

Mind-Blowing Extreme Sports Fact #36

MIND-BLOWING EXTREME SPORTS FACT #36

RIDING A BIKE ACROSS A CANYON GAP

In 2014, mountain biking legend **Andreu Lacondeguy** stunned the world by **clearing a 75-foot canyon gap** during the Red Bull Rampage in Utah.

Launching off a dirt cliff at high speed, Lacondeguy soared across the yawning gap with nothing but rock and air beneath him—**no safety nets, no second chances.** He stuck the landing perfectly, earning one of the highest scores in Rampage history.

It wasn't just a jump—it was defying gravity with two wheels and total belief.

Mind-Blowing Extreme Sports Fact #37

MIND-BLOWING EXTREME SPORTS FACT #37

THE RUNNER WHO CROSSED A CONTINENT

In 2013, Australian ultrarunner **Richard Bowles** ran the entire **3,300-mile length of the Great Himalaya Trail**—across **five countries** and some of the world's most punishing terrain.

Over five months, Bowles endured blizzards, landslides, altitude sickness, and extreme isolation. He averaged a marathon or more **every day**, sleeping in villages, tents, and sometimes caves.

It wasn't just a run—it was an odyssey through the spine of the Earth.

Mind-Blowing Extreme Sports Fact #38

MIND-BLOWING EXTREME SPORTS FACT #38

THE HIGHLINER WHO WALKED ABOVE RIO

In 2016, Brazilian slackliner **Renan Andrade** crossed a highline **between two cliffs overlooking Rio de Janeiro**, suspended hundreds of feet above the city's iconic coastline.

With Sugarloaf Mountain and the Atlantic Ocean as his backdrop, Andrade tiptoed across the thin line in gusty wind, **barefoot and without fear**, pausing mid-line to strike a yoga pose.

The balance, the bravery, the view—it was part art, part adrenaline, and 100% breathtaking.

Mind-Blowing Extreme Sports Fact #39

MIND-BLOWING EXTREME SPORTS FACT #39

THE MOTOCROSS LEAP OVER A FOOTBALL FIELD

In 2008, motocross legend **Robbie Maddison** launched off a massive ramp in Las Vegas and **jumped 322 feet through the air—the length of an entire football field**, plus extra.

He flew over the massive gap at nearly **90 mph**, landing cleanly on the other side with just inches to spare. The stunt shattered the world record for the longest motorcycle jump and became an instant classic in extreme sports history.

It wasn't just distance—it was flight fueled by throttle and guts.

Mind-Blowing Extreme Sports Fact #40

MIND-BLOWING EXTREME SPORTS FACT #40

KAYAKING THROUGH A GLACIAL ICE CAVE

In 2017, American adventurer **Erik Boomer** kayaked **deep inside a melting glacial ice cave** in Alaska, navigating narrow, freezing tunnels beneath a massive glacier.

The ice above him creaked and cracked, with massive chunks threatening to collapse at any moment. The water was icy, pitch black, and constantly shifting—but Boomer paddled on, exploring a world that few have ever seen *and even fewer have survived.*

It was part exploration, part escape room—inside a melting giant.

Mind-Blowing Extreme Sports Fact #41

MIND-BLOWING EXTREME SPORTS FACT #41

SNOWKITING ACROSS THE SOUTH POLE

In 2011, Norwegian explorer **Christian Eide** completed a **solo, unsupported trek to the South Pole**—using only skis and a snowkite.

Harnessing Antarctica's fierce winds, Eide glided across icy plains at speeds over **30 mph**, covering **700 miles in just 24 days**. He carried all his supplies, navigated whiteouts, and battled sub-zero temps—completely alone in one of the harshest places on Earth.

It wasn't just polar travel—it was *extreme survival with style.*

Mind-Blowing Extreme Sports Fact #42

MIND-BLOWING EXTREME SPORTS FACT #42

THE BAREFOOT CLIMB OF KILIMANJARO

In 2015, South African athlete **Khulekani Ngobese** scaled **Mount Kilimanjaro barefoot—all 19,341 feet of it.**

Braving razor-sharp rocks, freezing temperatures, and intense altitude shifts, Ngobese made the ascent without boots, socks, or even gloves. His goal wasn't just the summit—it was raising awareness for underprivileged children without proper footwear.

He didn't just conquer Africa's tallest peak—he did it with nothing but heart and soles.

Mind-Blowing Extreme Sports Fact #43

MIND-BLOWING EXTREME SPORTS FACT #43

CLIMBING A WATERFALL WITH NO ROPES

In 2013, British climber **Tim Emmett** completed the **first-ever free solo ice climb** of **Helmcken Falls** in Canada—**a 450-foot frozen waterfall** with ice formations unlike anywhere else.

The ice was fragile, overhanging, and constantly bombarded by spray from the roaring falls behind it, which refroze instantly—turning the climb into a vertical obstacle course of icicles and hanging daggers. And Emmett did it **without ropes.**

It was more than a climb—it was a frozen gauntlet of gravity and grit.

Mind-Blowing Extreme Sports Fact #44

MIND-BLOWING EXTREME SPORTS FACT #44

THE LONGEST UNDERWATER BIKE RIDE

In 2014, Slovenian athlete **Jure Škof** set a bizarre but brilliant record by **riding a bicycle underwater for over 3,000 feet**—nearly **two-thirds of a mile** beneath the surface of Lake Bled.

Wearing scuba gear and pedaling a specially weighted bike along the lakebed, Škof battled poor visibility, uneven terrain, and massive resistance with every turn of the wheels. It was part stunt, part endurance test, and all-in on creativity.

He didn't just ride—he redefined cycling's depth.

Mind-Blowing Extreme Sports Fact #45

MIND-BLOWING EXTREME SPORTS FACT #45

THE SKYDIVE INTO A VOLCANO CRATER

In 2015, Russian daredevil **Valery Rozov** BASE jumped **into the active Mutnovsky volcano** in Kamchatka, Russia—**parachuting straight into the crater**.

He leapt from a helicopter hovering above the steaming abyss, plunging through clouds of sulfur gas before deploying his chute and landing on a narrow patch inside the crater itself. The air was toxic, the winds unpredictable, and the margin for error nonexistent.

It wasn't just a jump—it was a dive into Earth's fury.

Mind-Blowing Extreme Sports Fact #46

MIND-BLOWING EXTREME SPORTS FACT #46

THE ULTRA SWIMMER WHO CROSSED FOUR CHANNELS

In 2017, American endurance swimmer **Sarah Thomas** became the **first person to swim across the English Channel four times in a row—without stopping.**

She swam **over 130 miles** in **54 straight hours**, through jellyfish stings, rough currents, and saltwater-induced nausea. Even more incredible? She completed the feat just a year after surviving breast cancer.

It wasn't just a swim—it was a defiant display of human resilience and raw determination.

Mind-Blowing Extreme Sports Fact #47

MIND-BLOWING EXTREME SPORTS FACT #47

SKATEBOARDING DOWN A 60-MPH HILL

In 2016, downhill skateboarder **Zak Maytum** bombed a hill in Colorado at a blistering **60 mph**, weaving through corners with **no guardrails and no room for error.**

Wearing only a helmet and leather suit, Maytum crouched low on his board, maintaining balance and control as the pavement blurred beneath him. Cars couldn't keep up—and even a tiny pebble could've spelled disaster.

It wasn't just fast—it was *gravity-fueled madness on four wheels.*

Mind-Blowing Extreme Sports Fact #48

MIND-BLOWING EXTREME SPORTS FACT #48

CLIMBING A SKYSCRAPER WITH SUCTION CUPS

In 2016, engineer and adventurer **Kyro Jeschke** scaled the **306-foot glass façade of the Frankfurt Tower** using **homemade vacuum suction cups**, inspired by *Spider-Man*.

Armed with nothing but his DIY gear and nerves of steel, he clung to the vertical glass, slowly ascending story by story without any safety harness. Every step was a test of pressure, grip, and guts.

It wasn't science fiction—it was suction-powered reality.

Mind-Blowing Extreme Sports Fact #49

MIND-BLOWING EXTREME SPORTS FACT #49

RUNNING A MARATHON IN THE SAHARA DESERT

The **Marathon des Sables** is widely known as the **toughest footrace on Earth**—a **156-mile ultra-marathon** run across the scorching **Sahara Desert** in temperatures exceeding **120°F**.

Athletes carry their own supplies, battle sandstorms, and endure brutal heat over six days of relentless terrain—dunes, salt flats, and rocky plains. Dehydration, heatstroke, and exhaustion are constant threats, yet hundreds line up every year.

It's not just a race—it's survival disguised as sport.

Mind-Blowing Extreme Sports Fact #50

MIND-BLOWING EXTREME SPORTS FACT #50

THE BASE JUMP FROM AN ICEBERG

In 2013, American wingsuit pilot **JT Holmes** completed the **first-ever BASE jump from a floating iceberg** off the coast of Baffin Island, Canada.

After scaling the towering ice formation—constantly shifting and cracking—Holmes leapt into the Arctic air in his wingsuit, gliding over freezing waters before deploying his parachute. The stunt was so dangerous that he had just minutes to act before the iceberg began to tilt and break apart.

It was the ultimate combination of precision, timing, and frozen chaos.

Mind-Blowing Extreme Sports Fact #51

MIND-BLOWING EXTREME SPORTS FACT #51

THE MAN WHO PARAGLIDED OVER EVEREST

In 2011, French adventurer **Babu Sunuwar** and Nepalese pilot **Lakpa Tsheri Sherpa** completed a world-first by **paragliding from the summit of Mount Everest.**

After reaching the 29,035-foot peak, they launched into the thin, freezing air with just a paraglider and a dream. They soared for **45 minutes**, descending safely into a lower valley—**skipping the treacherous two-day hike down.**

It wasn't just a descent—it was Everest's most epic exit.

Mind-Blowing Extreme Sports Fact #52

MIND-BLOWING EXTREME SPORTS FACT #52

SURFING INSIDE A LIVE HURRICANE

In 2019, pro surfer **Zane Schweitzer** paddled out to catch waves **during a Category 1 hurricane** off the coast of Florida—**on purpose.**

With winds topping 90 mph and ocean swells reaching 20 feet, Schweitzer navigated monstrous, churning waves in a storm most would flee from. The ride was violent, unpredictable, and borderline unrideable—**but he turned chaos into flow.**

It wasn't just surfing—it was riding nature's full fury.

Mind-Blowing Extreme Sports Fact #53

MIND-BLOWING EXTREME SPORTS FACT #53

THE LONGEST SLACKLINE WALK OVER WATER

In 2020, German slackliner **Friedi Kühne** set a world record by walking a **2,800-foot slackline** stretched high above a lake in Brazil—**the longest water-crossing ever on a slackline.**

Suspended hundreds of feet in the air with only a 1-inch line beneath him, Kühne took thousands of careful steps, battling wind, sway, and exhaustion over the course of **an hour-long crossing.**

It wasn't just balance—it was a marathon in the sky.

Mind-Blowing Extreme Sports Fact #54

MIND-BLOWING EXTREME SPORTS FACT #54

THE SKIER WHO LAUNCHED OFF A CLIFF BLINDFOLDED

In 2014, pro skier **JP Auclair** stunned viewers in a short film where he **skied backward, spun 360s, and even launched off a cliff—all while blindfolded.**

Filmed as part of an artistic project blending creativity and extreme skill, the stunt required total spatial awareness, flawless terrain memory, and next-level confidence. One wrong move meant a fall—or far worse.

It wasn't just a trick—it was skiing on instinct and style.

Mind-Blowing Extreme Sports Fact #55

RUNNING A MARATHON... IN A VOLCANO

In 2017, over 100 daring athletes participated in the **Volcano Marathon** in Chile, racing at over **14,000 feet of elevation—inside the Atacama Desert's volcanic field.**

The course wound through ash, lava rock, and thin air near active volcanoes, with blistering sun and frigid winds trading off throughout the race. Oxygen was scarce, footing was brutal, and every step felt like running on Mars.

It wasn't just a marathon—it was *lava, lungs, and lunacy.*

Mind-Blowing Extreme Sports Fact #56

MIND-BLOWING EXTREME SPORTS FACT #56

THE BMX TRICK THAT DEFIED PHYSICS

In 2019, Australian BMX rider **Ryan Williams** landed the world's first **triple frontflip** on a BMX bike—**a trick long thought impossible.**

He launched off a mega ramp, flipped forward **three full times** in the air, and somehow landed cleanly on two wheels. The timing, speed, and body control required were mind-boggling, and even seasoned pros called it "insane."

It wasn't just a trick—it was BMX wizardry in midair.

Mind-Blowing Extreme Sports Fact #57

MIND-BLOWING EXTREME SPORTS FACT #57

THE LONGEST UNDERWATER BREATH HOLD

In 2021, Croatian freediver **Budimir Šobat** shattered records by holding his breath underwater for **24 minutes and 37 seconds—the longest static apnea ever recorded.**

Before the attempt, he hyperventilated with pure oxygen to fully saturate his blood. Even so, the feat required total stillness, intense focus, and an almost meditative control over the body's urge to breathe.

It wasn't just breath-holding—it was a deep dive into human potential.

Mind-Blowing Extreme Sports Fact #58

MIND-BLOWING EXTREME SPORTS FACT #58

PARACHUTING INTO A SOCCER STADIUM

In 2014, stuntman **Mario Fuchs** stunned fans by **skydiving into the Allianz Arena in Munich—landing on the field moments before kickoff.**

Jumping from a helicopter high above the stadium, Fuchs navigated swirling wind currents and a tight landing zone surrounded by 70,000 spectators. With perfect precision, he touched down at midfield, delivering the match ball like a human missile.

It wasn't just a stunt—it was sports delivery, extreme edition.

Mind-Blowing Extreme Sports Fact #59

MIND-BLOWING EXTREME SPORTS FACT #59

THE CLIMBER WHO HUNG FROM A FLYING HELICOPTER

In 2018, Swiss alpinist **Nicolas Hojac** took extreme to new heights by **hanging from a helicopter's landing skid—with one hand, no harness, and thousands of feet of air below.**

Part of a high-altitude stunt over the Swiss Alps, Hojac gripped the skid as the chopper banked and spun, with only raw strength and mental steel keeping him in the sky. The entire sequence lasted just seconds—but felt like forever.

It wasn't just climbing—it was flight by fingertips.

Mind-Blowing Extreme Sports Fact #60

MIND-BLOWING EXTREME SPORTS FACT #60

THE SNOWBOARDER WHO RODE AN ACTIVE VOLCANO

In 2016, pro snowboarder **Mitch Tölderer** descended **Volcán Villarrica** in Chile—**while it was actively erupting.**

With ash billowing behind him and lava glowing at the crater, Tölderer carved down its steep, unstable slopes covered in a thin layer of snow. The terrain was unpredictable, the air toxic, and the margin for error razor-thin—but the footage was unforgettable.

It wasn't just snowboarding—it was surfing fire on a frozen wave.

Mind-Blowing Extreme Sports Fact #61

MIND-BLOWING EXTREME SPORTS FACT #61

THE ICE SWIMMER WHO DOVE BELOW THE ARCTIC

In 2021, Finnish swimmer **Johanna Nordblad** set a world record by **swimming 103 meters (338 feet) under ice—in a frozen lake, wearing no wetsuit.**

With only a swimsuit, goggles, and a single breath, she glided beneath a solid sheet of ice in water just above freezing. Visibility was near zero, and she had to navigate by counting strokes to find the exit hole—**one mistake, and she wouldn't surface.**

It wasn't just cold—it was ice-blooded endurance at its peak.

Mind-Blowing Extreme Sports Fact #62

MIND-BLOWING EXTREME SPORTS FACT #62

JUMPING A DIRT BIKE ONTO A MOVING TRAIN

In 2017, Australian stunt rider **Robbie Maddison** pulled off a cinematic stunt for the ages: **he jumped a dirt bike onto a moving train**, then **jumped off it again**—all at full speed.

Timing was everything. He launched off a dirt ramp, landed perfectly on a train car barreling down the tracks, rode a few cars' length, then *launched again* off a second ramp onto solid ground.

It wasn't just a jump—it was a two-part masterpiece of mayhem.

Mind-Blowing Extreme Sports Fact #63

MIND-BLOWING EXTREME SPORTS FACT #63

RUNNING ACROSS AN ENTIRE FROZEN LAKE

In 2019, endurance runner **Michael Wardian** completed a **135-mile ultramarathon across Lake Khövsgöl** in Mongolia—**completely frozen over.**

With windchill temperatures plunging below **-40°F**, he ran for over **two days straight**, battling frostbite, blisters, and hallucinations from sleep deprivation. The ice cracked beneath him at times, and snowstorms rolled in without warning.

It wasn't just a run—it was an arctic odyssey on foot.

Mind-Blowing Extreme Sports Fact #64

MIND-BLOWING EXTREME SPORTS FACT #64

THE HIGH-DIVE FROM A HELICOPTER

In 2015, Colombian cliff diver **Orlando Duque** made history (again) by **leaping from a helicopter at 75 feet**—into a narrow inlet in Chile's Pacific waters.

Hovering high above the rugged coastline, Duque timed the jump perfectly, launching himself in a clean vertical dive into a tight splash zone surrounded by rocks. One misjudged gust of wind or tilt of the chopper, and the stunt could've ended in disaster.

It wasn't just high diving—it was aerial artistry in motion.

Mind-Blowing Extreme Sports Fact #65

MIND-BLOWING EXTREME SPORTS FACT #65

THE URBAN CLIMBER WHO HUNG BY ONE HAND

In 2017, Russian daredevil **Vitali Raskalov** scaled the **Shenzhen Center**—one of China's tallest skyscrapers—and **hung by one hand from its spire**, over **1,700 feet above the ground.**

With no ropes, harness, or safety net, he climbed the building illegally, then casually dangled over the city, capturing the moment with a selfie stick. The video went viral—and so did viewers' heart rates.

It wasn't just urban exploration—it was gravity-defying madness.

Mind-Blowing Extreme Sports Fact #66

MIND-BLOWING EXTREME SPORTS FACT #66

SANDBOARDING DOWN A LIVE VOLCANO

In Nicaragua, thrill-seekers flock to **Cerro Negro**, one of the world's most active volcanoes, to try an insane sport: **volcano boarding.**

Riders hike up the black, ash-covered slope, then launch themselves downhill on reinforced boards, reaching speeds of up to **55 mph**—all while dodging sharp volcanic rocks and clouds of sulfur gas. One wrong lean, and it's a face-first slide into lava gravel.

It's not just boarding—it's surfing the Earth's fire.

Mind-Blowing Extreme Sports Fact #67

MIND-BLOWING EXTREME SPORTS FACT #67

THE WINDSURFER WHO CROSSED THE ATLANTIC

In 2013, French adventurer **Raphaël Domjan** became the first person to **windsurf across the Atlantic Ocean using only solar power**—and he did it solo.

Starting from Las Palmas in the Canary Islands, he crossed over **3,000 miles** of open ocean aboard a custom solar-powered trimaran, using a windsurf sail to harness both wind and sun. Battling storms, equipment failures, and total isolation, he reached Guadeloupe after weeks at sea.

It wasn't just windsurfing—it was a renewable-powered odyssey.

Mind-Blowing Extreme Sports Fact #68

MIND-BLOWING EXTREME SPORTS FACT #68

THE SKIER WHO BACKFLIPPED OFF A CLIFF

In 2010, Swedish freestyle skier **Jon Olsson** stunned the skiing world by **landing a perfect backflip off a 100-foot cliff** in the Alps—**wearing a full camera rig.**

He approached the drop at high speed, launched into the flip with flawless form, and touched down in deep powder like it was just another trick in the park. The stunt blended big-mountain danger with freestyle flair—and the footage went viral.

It wasn't just a flip—it was high-altitude artistry in motion.

Mind-Blowing Extreme Sports Fact #69

MIND-BLOWING EXTREME SPORTS FACT #69

THE MAN WHO RAN A MARATHON BACKWARD

In 2004, German athlete **Markus Jürgens** completed an entire **marathon running backward**—and later broke the world record by finishing one in **3 hours and 38 minutes.**

Jürgens trained his body and brain to run in reverse, mastering balance, pacing, and terrain awareness without the ability to see where he was going. Spectators were stunned as he crossed the finish line *facing the wrong way—but leading the pack.*

It wasn't just running—it was flipping the sport on its head.

Mind-Blowing Extreme Sports Fact #70

MIND-BLOWING EXTREME SPORTS FACT #70

RIDING A ZIPLINE AT 100 MPH

In 2018, thrill-seekers lined up for **"Velocity 2"** in Wales—**the fastest zipline in the world**, where riders soar at over **100 mph** across a vast quarry.

Suspended in a superhero-style harness, riders launch from a mountain-top platform and fly **1.5 kilometers** over cliffs, lakes, and rocky terrain, just feet above the ground at times. The experience is so fast, goggles are required—*not for style, but survival.*

It's not just a zipline—it's a flight without wings.

Mind-Blowing Extreme Sports Fact #71

MIND-BLOWING EXTREME SPORTS FACT #71

THE CYCLIST WHO RODE THE DEATH ROAD

In Bolivia, adrenaline junkies travel from around the world to bike down **Yungas Road**—infamously known as **"Death Road."**

Stretching 40 miles through the Andes, it features **3,600-foot drop-offs, no guardrails**, and blind corners slicked with mist. Despite the danger, riders descend this narrow dirt track at high speeds, balancing thrill with sheer terror.

It's not just mountain biking—it's a ride along the edge of oblivion.

Mind-Blowing Extreme Sports Fact #72

MIND-BLOWING EXTREME SPORTS FACT #72

THE FIRST SKYDIVE WITHOUT A PARACHUTE

In 2016, stuntman **Luke Aikins** made history by becoming the **first person to skydive from 25,000 feet with no parachute—and survive.**

Wearing only a tracking suit, Aikins plummeted at terminal velocity and landed **in a 100-by-100-foot net** suspended 20 stories high. The margin for error was microscopic—*he had to hit the center perfectly or miss the net entirely.*

It wasn't just a skydive—it was a calculated plunge into legend.

Mind-Blowing Extreme Sports Fact #73

MIND-BLOWING EXTREME SPORTS FACT #73

THE CLIMBER WHO SLEPT ON A CLIFF

Extreme climbers like **Emily Harrington** and **Tommy Caldwell** have taken multi-day climbs to new extremes by **sleeping in "portaledges"**—tiny tents hanging thousands of feet above the ground.

These suspended shelters cling to sheer rock faces like hammocks bolted to the sky. Climbers eat, rest, and sleep with nothing but thin fabric between them and a vertical drop—often in wild weather and total darkness.

It's not just camping—it's cliffside survival in midair.

Mind-Blowing Extreme Sports Fact #74

MIND-BLOWING EXTREME SPORTS FACT #74

RUNNING A MARATHON IN THE NORTH POLE

Yes, it's real—the **North Pole Marathon** challenges runners to complete **26.2 miles on floating ice**, in temperatures below **-30°F**, with armed guards nearby to protect against polar bears.

Athletes wear layers of insulated gear, run through snowdrifts and slush, and often battle fierce winds that feel like knives. Footing is unpredictable, the course shifts with the ice, and even GPS struggles to work that far north.

It's not just extreme—it's *frostbitten endurance at the top of the world.*

Mind-Blowing Extreme Sports Fact #75

MIND-BLOWING EXTREME SPORTS FACT #75

THE LONGEST FREE SOLO SLACKLINE WALK

In 2016, German slackliner **Alexander Schulz** walked a **2,460-foot slackline—without any safety tether**—hundreds of feet above a canyon in China.

With only his balance and mental focus to rely on, Schulz tiptoed across the narrow webbing for nearly an hour, exposed to wind, nerves, and the sheer drop below. One misstep would have meant instant freefall.

It wasn't just walking a line—it was defying death with every step.

100 MIND-BLOWING EXTREME SPORTS FACTS

Mind-Blowing Extreme Sports Fact #76

SNOWMOBILING ACROSS THE ARCTIC OCEAN

In 2015, Norwegian adventurer **Børge Ousland** crossed parts of the **frozen Arctic Ocean on a snowmobile**, braving shifting ice sheets, crevasses, and open water leads.

The journey spanned hundreds of miles over unstable, drifting terrain where a wrong turn could plunge rider and machine into freezing depths. With temperatures dipping below -50°F, Ousland relied on satellite navigation and survival instincts to make it through.

It wasn't just a ride—it was mechanized madness on the edge of the world.

Mind-Blowing Extreme Sports Fact #77

MIND-BLOWING EXTREME SPORTS FACT #77

BASE JUMPING INTO AN UNDERGROUND CAVE

In 2012, wingsuit pilot **Cedric Dumont** leapt into Mexico's **Cave of Swallows**—a giant vertical shaft so deep, it could swallow the Statue of Liberty.

He launched from the jungle-covered rim and plummeted into the darkness, freefalling **over 1,200 feet** before deploying his parachute just above the cave floor. The descent lasted seconds, but the visual of a human diving into the Earth's core was unforgettable.

It wasn't just BASE jumping—it was a plunge into the planet.

Mind-Blowing Extreme Sports Fact #78

MIND-BLOWING EXTREME SPORTS FACT #78

RIDING A MOUNTAIN BIKE ACROSS A CRANE

In 2020, Scottish trials rider **Danny MacAskill** took balance to a new level by **riding his mountain bike across a construction crane—hundreds of feet above the ground.**

The beam was barely wider than his tires, swaying slightly in the wind, with a jaw-dropping drop on either side. With surgical precision, MacAskill pedaled across the steel arm, even pausing mid-line to pop a wheelie.

It wasn't just biking—it was tightrope artistry on two wheels.

Mind-Blowing Extreme Sports Fact #79

MIND-BLOWING EXTREME SPORTS FACT #79

THE LONGEST SWIM IN A RIVER

In 2007, Slovenian swimmer **Martin Strel** completed a mind-blowing feat: he **swam the entire length of the Amazon River—3,273 miles**—in just **66 days.**

He faced piranhas, crocodiles, parasites, and river-borne infections, swimming up to **10 hours a day** in dangerous, murky waters. At times delirious from heat and exhaustion, he kept going with one goal: to raise awareness for clean water access.

It wasn't just a swim—it was a battle against nature's wildest current.

Mind-Blowing Extreme Sports Fact #80

MIND-BLOWING EXTREME SPORTS FACT #80

THE SKATER WHO DID A LOOP ON A SKYBRIDGE

In 2015, pro skater **Tony Hawk** stunned the world once again by completing a **full vertical loop** on a custom-built **skybridge—hundreds of feet in the air**, with only a guardrail and guts.

The loop was narrow, fast, and perched on an open-air platform with dizzying views below. One slip meant falling—not just off the board, but potentially off the edge. Hawk nailed it with his signature cool, adding one more first to his legendary résumé.

It wasn't just a trick—it was history carved in concrete and courage.

Mind-Blowing Extreme Sports Fact #81

MIND-BLOWING EXTREME SPORTS FACT #81

SURFING A WAVE FOR OVER 3 MINUTES

In 2011, surfer **Gary Saavedra** rode a **man-made river wave in Panama** for an astonishing **3 minutes and 55 seconds**, covering over **2 miles**—setting a Guinness World Record for the **longest time and distance surfed.**

The wave was created by a speedboat on the Gatun Lake section of the Panama Canal. Saavedra balanced, adjusted, and carved non-stop, fighting leg burn and wave fatigue for nearly 4 straight minutes.

It wasn't ocean surfing—it was endurance surfing at its finest.

Mind-Blowing Extreme Sports Fact #82

MIND-BLOWING EXTREME SPORTS FACT #82

THE WINGSUIT PILOT WHO FLEW THROUGH A RING

In 2016, Italian wingsuit flyer **Uli Emanuele** stunned the world by **flying through a tiny rock arch—just over 6 feet wide**—at over **100 mph.**

Wearing a wingsuit and a helmet cam, he launched from a mountain, navigated a narrow flight path through the Alps, and **threaded himself through the hole in the rock** with only inches to spare on either side.

It wasn't just precision—it was aerial surgery at terminal velocity.

Mind-Blowing Extreme Sports Fact #83

MIND-BLOWING EXTREME SPORTS FACT #83

ICE CLIMBING A MELTING GLACIER ARCH

In 2019, climber **Will Gadd** returned to **the Athabasca Glacier** in Canada to scale a **massive ice arch—knowing it was rapidly melting beneath him.**

The arch was delicate, unstable, and unpredictable. Every axe swing had to be perfect, as chunks of ice were constantly falling around him. Scientists warned the formation wouldn't last much longer—and days later, it collapsed.

It wasn't just a climb—it was a farewell ascent to a vanishing world.

Mind-Blowing Extreme Sports Fact #84

MIND-BLOWING EXTREME SPORTS FACT #84

THE ULTRA RACE THROUGH A JUNGLE

The **Jungle Ultra** in Peru is one of the world's most brutal footraces—**a 143-mile run through the Amazon rainforest**, complete with mud, heat, and wildlife.

Runners carry all their own gear and race across rivers, up slippery hills, and through dense vegetation in **100% humidity**, all while avoiding snakes, spiders, and exhaustion. Finishers call it a battle of **mind over mud.**

It's not just a run—it's survival disguised as a race.

Mind-Blowing Extreme Sports Fact #85

MIND-BLOWING EXTREME SPORTS FACT #85

THE SKYDIVE WITH A STUNT PLANE LOOP

In 2014, daredevil **Wojtek Czyz** pulled off a jaw-dropping feat: he **jumped from a stunt plane mid-loop**, freefalling as the aircraft inverted above him.

The plane performed a vertical loop, and Czyz timed his jump to coincide with the top of the arc—**creating the illusion that he was outrunning the aircraft midair.** The precision needed was unreal, with pilot and jumper perfectly in sync.

It wasn't just a jump—it was sky choreography at its wildest.

Mind-Blowing Extreme Sports Fact #86

MIND-BLOWING EXTREME SPORTS FACT #86

CLIMBING A DAM WITH BARE HANDS

In 2011, Czech climber **Adam Ondra** scaled the **418-foot Verzasca Dam** in Switzerland—using no ropes, no safety gear, and no climbing shoes.

The dam's concrete surface offered barely any grip, but Ondra relied on tiny imperfections, raw finger strength, and flawless technique to ascend what looked like a vertical wall of smooth stone.

It wasn't a mountain—it was man versus gravity on a man-made monolith.

Mind-Blowing Extreme Sports Fact #87

MIND-BLOWING EXTREME SPORTS FACT #87

RIDING A JET SKI ACROSS THE ATLANTIC

In 2006, Spanish adventurer **Alvaro de Marichalar** completed a **transatlantic crossing on a jet ski**, traveling **10,000 miles over open ocean—alone**.

He rode a tiny 9-foot watercraft through storms, high waves, and scorching sun, stopping only to refuel from a support boat and sleeping on the jet ski itself. The journey took **more than three months**, testing his endurance and willpower every mile.

It wasn't just a ride—it was a solo surf across the sea.

Mind-Blowing Extreme Sports Fact #88

MIND-BLOWING EXTREME SPORTS FACT #88

THE SKIER WHO JUMPED OVER A ROAD

In 2016, French freestyle skier **Candide Thovex** wowed the internet by **jumping a busy mountain road—without snow.**

In a viral video, Thovex carved through grassy slopes, forests, and dirt paths, then launched off a natural bump and **cleared an entire two-lane road**, just as a car passed underneath. His skis never touched snow once— *yet he made it look effortless.*

It wasn't just skiing—it was redefining what skis were meant for.

Mind-Blowing Extreme Sports Fact #89

MIND-BLOWING EXTREME SPORTS FACT #89

PADDLEBOARDING AROUND AN ENTIRE COUNTRY

In 2018, British adventurer **Brendon Prince** set out to **circumnavigate mainland Britain on a stand-up paddleboard**—and succeeded, becoming the **first person to do so.**

He paddled over **2,500 miles** through rough seas, unpredictable tides, and stormy weather, all while standing upright. The journey took **141 days**, tested every muscle in his body, and raised awareness for water safety and mental health.

It wasn't just paddleboarding—it was coastal conquest by core strength.

Mind-Blowing Extreme Sports Fact #90

MIND-BLOWING EXTREME SPORTS FACT #90

THE LONGEST HIGHLINE OVER ACTIVE TRAFFIC

In 2015, French highliner **Nathan Paulin** walked a **1,000-foot slackline** stretched over the **busy Aiguille du Midi cable car route** in the French Alps—**with gondolas zipping beneath him.**

Balancing thousands of feet above the valley floor, Paulin calmly crossed the line while tourists watched in awe from inside the moving cars. The wind was unpredictable, the exposure dizzying, and yet he made it look serene.

It wasn't just balance—it was ballet above a highway in the sky.

Mind-Blowing Extreme Sports Fact #91

MIND-BLOWING EXTREME SPORTS FACT #91

CLIFF DIVING FROM A HOT AIR BALLOON

In 2018, Austrian diver **Laso Schaller** took cliff diving to new heights—literally—by **jumping from a hot air balloon into a lake** from over **190 feet in the air.**

With no platform and nothing solid beneath him, Schaller launched into a full dive mid-flight, freefalling for nearly **3 seconds** before hitting the water with perfect form. It was one of the highest controlled dives ever attempted.

It wasn't just diving—it was a leap from the clouds.

Mind-Blowing Extreme Sports Fact #92

MIND-BLOWING EXTREME SPORTS FACT #92

THE ULTRA CYCLIST WHO RODE AROUND THE WORLD

In 2017, Scottish cyclist **Mark Beaumont** shattered records by **cycling around the world in just 78 days—averaging 240 miles per day.**

He crossed continents, battled wild weather, dodged traffic in remote regions, and kept a schedule so intense he barely slept. From the deserts of Australia to the mountains of Europe, he pedaled through pain, exhaustion, and jet lag to circle the planet.

It wasn't just a ride—it was global domination on two wheels.

Mind-Blowing Extreme Sports Fact #93

MIND-BLOWING EXTREME SPORTS FACT #93

CLIMBING AN ICEBERG WITH ICE AXES ONLY

In 2015, American climber **Klemen Premrl** completed a first-of-its-kind ascent—**scaling a floating iceberg in the Arctic Ocean using only ice axes and crampons.**

The berg shifted constantly with the waves, making it feel like climbing a moving mountain. Every swing had to be fast and accurate, or the fragile ice could shear away. And if he fell? It was straight into freezing water.

It wasn't just ice climbing—it was vertical chaos on a drifting sculpture.

Mind-Blowing Extreme Sports Fact #94

MIND-BLOWING EXTREME SPORTS FACT #94

KAYAKING OFF A SNOW-COVERED CLIFF

In 2013, pro kayaker **Aniol Serrasolses** pulled off a wild stunt by **launching his kayak off a snowy mountain cliff—landing directly into a river below.**

Wearing ski gear and gripping his paddle, he rocketed down a snowy slope, hit the edge at full speed, and dropped dozens of feet into icy, rushing water—seamlessly transitioning from snow to whitewater in seconds.

It wasn't just a drop—it was a winter-to-water thrill ride.

Mind-Blowing Extreme Sports Fact #95

MIND-BLOWING EXTREME SPORTS FACT #95

THE BASE JUMP OFF A MOVING TRUCK

In 2015, wingsuit flyer **Miles Daisher** pulled off a stunt straight out of an action film: he **BASE jumped off a moving semi-truck driving across a bridge.**

As the truck sped along at over 50 mph, Daisher climbed to the roof, waited for the perfect moment, and launched into the air—**soaring off the bridge and into the canyon below** before deploying his parachute.

It wasn't just timing—it was precision at highway speed.

Mind-Blowing Extreme Sports Fact #96

MIND-BLOWING EXTREME SPORTS FACT #96

THE DEEPEST SCUBA DIVE EVER RECORDED

In 2014, Egyptian diver **Ahmed Gabr** set the world record for the **deepest scuba dive**, plunging to an astonishing **1,090 feet**—deeper than the Eiffel Tower is tall.

The descent took just **12 minutes**, but the return to the surface required over **15 hours**, due to carefully planned decompression stops to avoid deadly nitrogen buildup. He trained for years, knowing that even a small mistake at that depth could be fatal.

It wasn't just a dive—it was a journey to the ocean's edge.

Mind-Blowing Extreme Sports Fact #97

MIND-BLOWING EXTREME SPORTS FACT #97

RIDING A UNICYCLE ACROSS A CANYON

In 2019, extreme unicyclist **Lutz Eichholz** took balance to the limit by **riding a unicycle across a narrow canyon ridge—with sheer drops on both sides.**

The path was barely wider than his tire, the wind unpredictable, and there was no safety net—just laser focus and leg control. One twitch in either direction, and it would've been a fall into hundreds of feet of open air.

It wasn't just balance—it was bravery on one wheel.

Mind-Blowing Extreme Sports Fact #98

MIND-BLOWING EXTREME SPORTS FACT #98

THE LONGEST SWIM IN ANTARCTICA

In 2020, British endurance swimmer **Lewis Pugh** became the first person to **swim a full kilometer in the Antarctic Ocean, wearing only a speedo, cap, and goggles.**

He plunged into the **28.8°F (-1.8°C) water** near melting glaciers to highlight the climate crisis, braving icebergs, freezing currents, and the threat of cold shock with no thermal protection. The swim took just under 20 minutes—but pushed human limits to the brink.

It wasn't just cold—it was courage in its rawest form.

Mind-Blowing Extreme Sports Fact #99

MIND-BLOWING EXTREME SPORTS FACT #99

THE SKATER WHO LANDED THE FIRST 1080

In 2012, at just 12 years old, **Tom Schaar** made skateboarding history by **landing the world's first 1080—three full spins in the air**—on a mega ramp in California.

No one had ever landed the trick before, not even the pros. Schaar built up massive speed, launched into the sky, spun three times with flawless form, and stomped the landing like a seasoned veteran.

It wasn't just a trick—it was a turning point in skateboarding evolution.

# Mind-Blowing Extreme Sports Fact #100

MIND-BLOWING EXTREME SPORTS FACT #100

THE ULTIMATE TRIATHLON ACROSS CONTINENTS

In 2021, French adventurer **Guillaume Néry** completed a one-of-a-kind triathlon: **swimming, biking, and running across three continents in a single day.**

He began with an ocean swim in Asia, cycled across a rugged Middle Eastern desert, then sprinted across Europe's border to finish—**all within 24 hours.** Each leg was extreme on its own, but together? A global endurance masterpiece.

It wasn't just a triathlon—it was a border-breaking feat of human will.

CONCLUSION

Congratulations! You've just powered through *100 Mind-Blowing Extreme Sports Facts*—a whirlwind tour through some of the boldest, wildest, and most death-defying feats ever attempted by humans. From mid-air flips to freezing swims, sky-high stunts to ultra-endurance challenges, you've seen just how far the human spirit can go when fear takes a back seat to passion.

But here's the thing about extreme sports—they're constantly evolving. New records are set, new limits are tested, and new adventurers are always pushing the boundaries of what we thought was possible. For every story in this book, there are hundreds more out there just waiting to unfold—on mountaintops, in oceans, across deserts, and even in the sky.

Maybe this collection has inspired a bit of awe. Maybe it sparked your curiosity about a sport you'd never heard of. Or maybe it just gave you a fresh appreciation for what people can do when they mix skill, courage, and just a touch of madness.

One thing's for sure: the world of extreme sports never stands still. So as you close this book, don't think of it as the end—think of it as the launch pad for your next adrenaline-fueled rabbit hole.

Until next time, stay curious, stay bold, and remember: the most mind-blowing feats are the ones no one's dared to try... yet.

ACKNOWLEDGEMENTS

Creating *100 Mind-Blowing Extreme Sports Facts* has been an exhilarating ride—full of late nights, wild research rabbit holes, and more "Wait, *they* did *what*?" moments than I can count. While my name might be on the cover, this book wouldn't exist without the incredible people who helped bring it to life.

First, a massive thank you to the fearless athletes, filmmakers, and storytellers who capture and share these jaw-dropping feats. Your courage, creativity, and commitment to the edge of possibility are what inspired every single page. This book is a tribute to your relentless pursuit of the extraordinary.

To my family and friends—you've cheered me on through every twist, turn, and high-speed sprint toward the finish line. Thanks for letting me talk endlessly about volcano dives, ice swims, and canyon flips over dinner. Your support means everything.

To my readers—thank you for being bold enough to join me on this wild journey. Whether you're here for the adrenaline rush, the unbelievable facts, or just a break from the ordinary, this book was made for you. Your curiosity fuels the next chapter.

And finally, to the world of extreme sports itself—thank you for being so endlessly daring. You've given us more than just stunts and records—you've given us a reminder that limits are meant to be pushed.

Here's to the fearless, the dreamers, and the ones who never say "That's impossible."

ABOUT THE AUTHOR

Felix Grayson is a storyteller at heart, driven by a deep curiosity for the strange, surprising, and downright unbelievable moments that push human limits. With a passion for uncovering the wildest feats in extreme sports, Felix created *100 Mind-Blowing Extreme Sports Facts* to entertain, inspire, and leave readers asking, "Wait… they actually did that?"

When he's not chasing stories of high-altitude stunts, underwater adventures, or gravity-defying tricks, Felix enjoys exploring remote corners of the world, devouring adventure documentaries, and pondering life's big questions over a strong cup of coffee and the sound of GoPro footage in the background. A firm believer in fearless storytelling and the thrill of the unknown, Felix invites you to ride through the edge of what's possible—because the greatest stories are the ones that leave your jaw on the floor.

www.ingramcontent.com/pod-product-compliance
Lightning Source LLC
Chambersburg PA
CBHW030318080526
44584CB00012B/614